animal planet

Wild About ANIMALS

COLORING BOOK

THUNDER BAY
P·R·E·S·S

San Diego, California

Thunder Bay Press
An imprint of Printers Row Publishing Group
9717 Pacific Heights Blvd, San Diego, CA 92121
www.thunderbaybooks.com • mail@thunderbaybooks.com

2021© Discovery Communications, LLC. Animal Planet ™
and logo are trademarks of Discovery Communications, LLC,
used under license. All rights reserved. animalplanet.com

Printers Row Publishing Group is a division of Readerlink Distribution Services, LLC.
Thunder Bay Press is a registered trademark of Readerlink Distribution Services, LLC.

Correspondence regarding the content of this book should be sent to Thunder Bay Press,
Editorial Department, at the above address.

Thunder Bay Press
Publisher: Peter Norton
Associate Publisher: Ana Parker
Senior Developmental Editor: April Graham Farr
Developmental Editor: Diane Cain
Editor: Jessica Matteson
Editorial Assistant: Sarah Fagaly
Production Team: Rusty von Dyl, Beno Chan, Mimi Oey

ISBN: 978-1-64517-429-5

Printed in China.

25 24 23 22 21   2 3 4 5 6

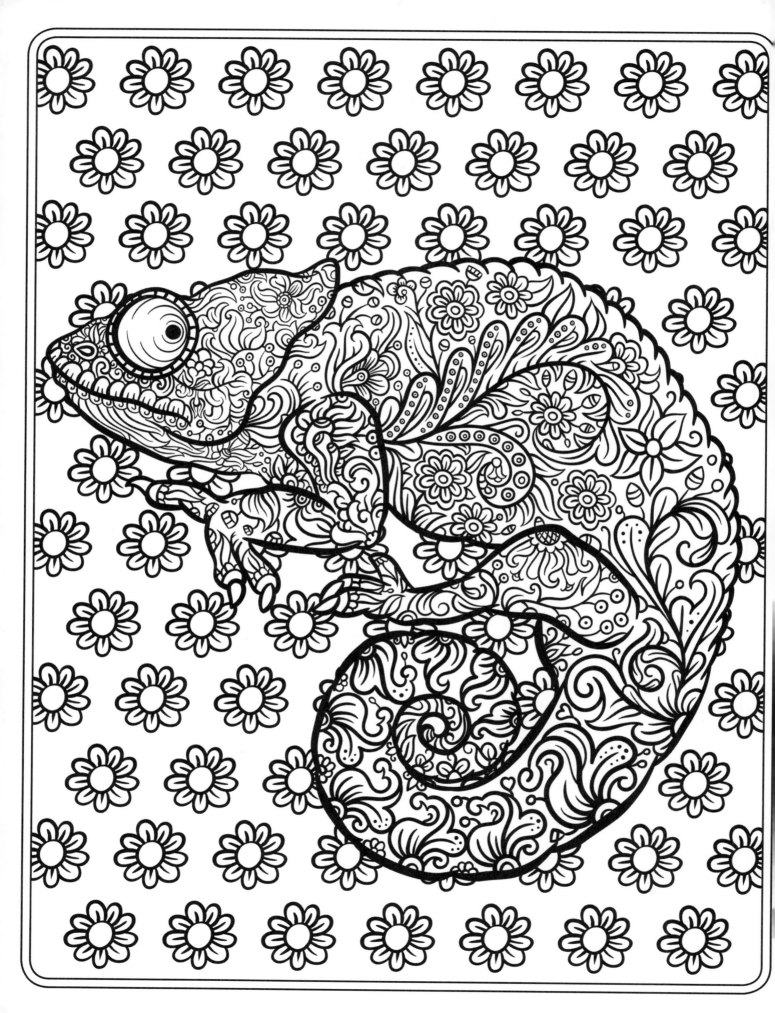

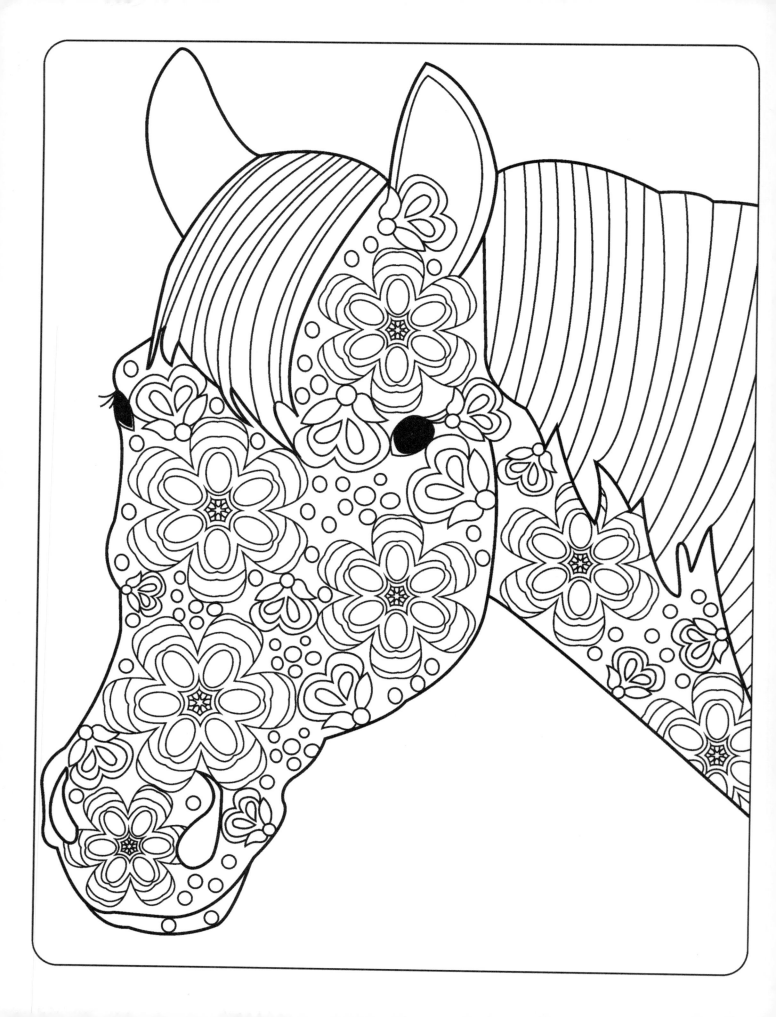

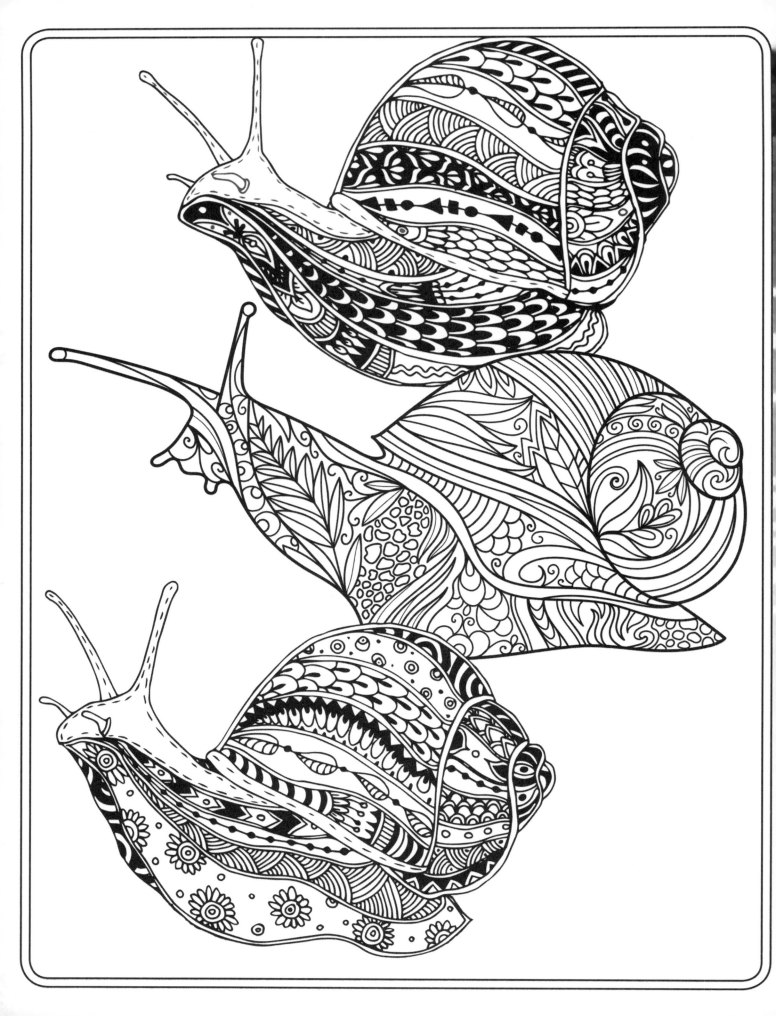

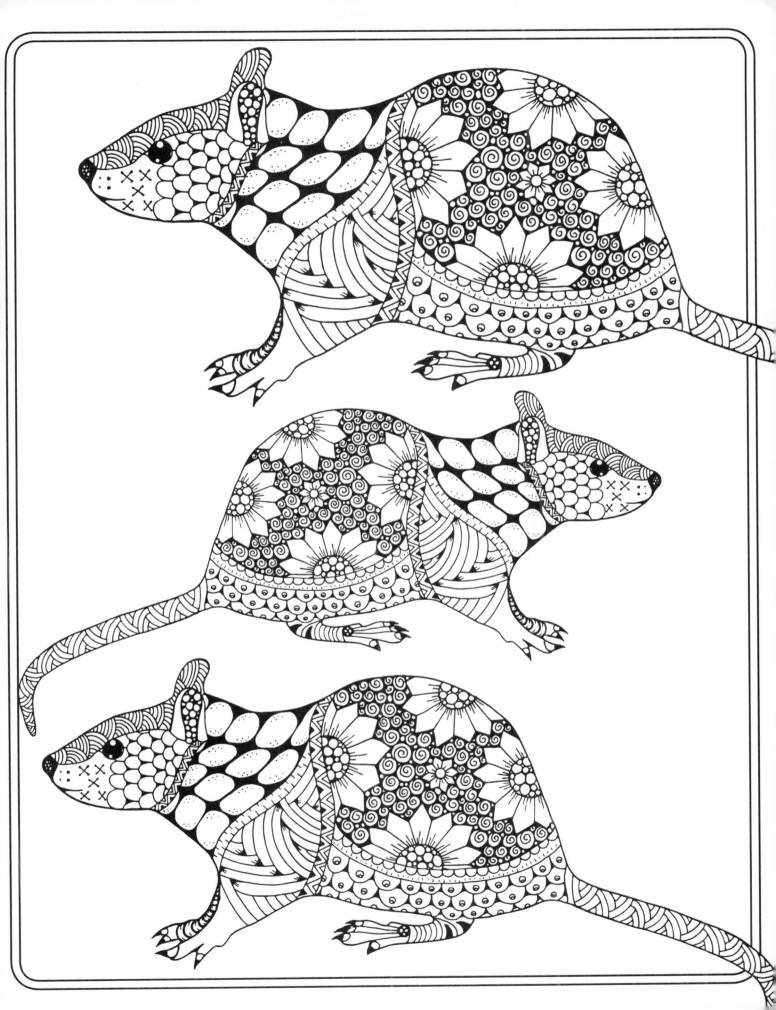

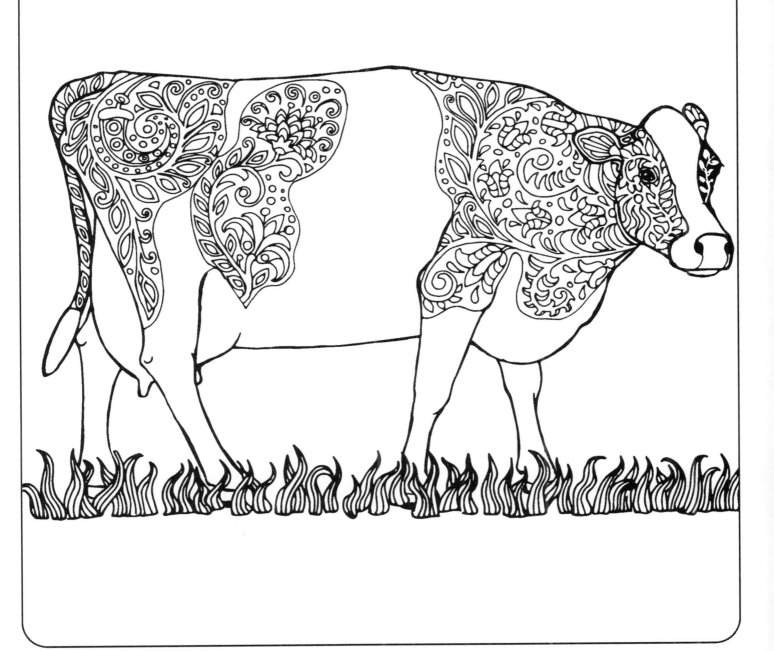

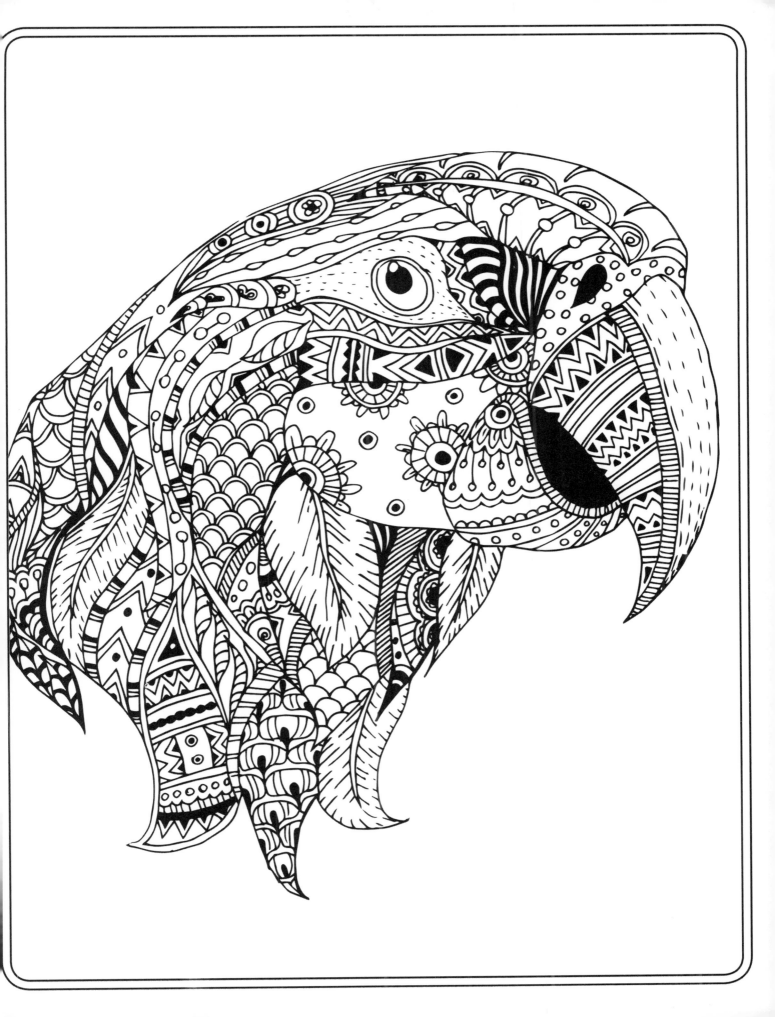

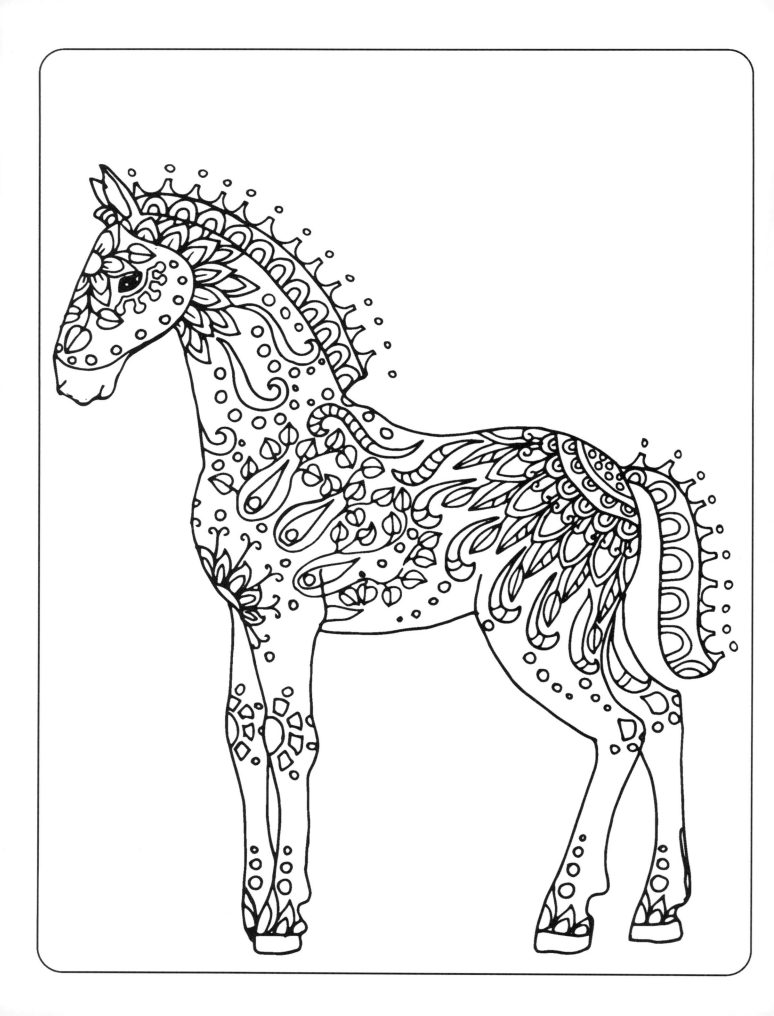

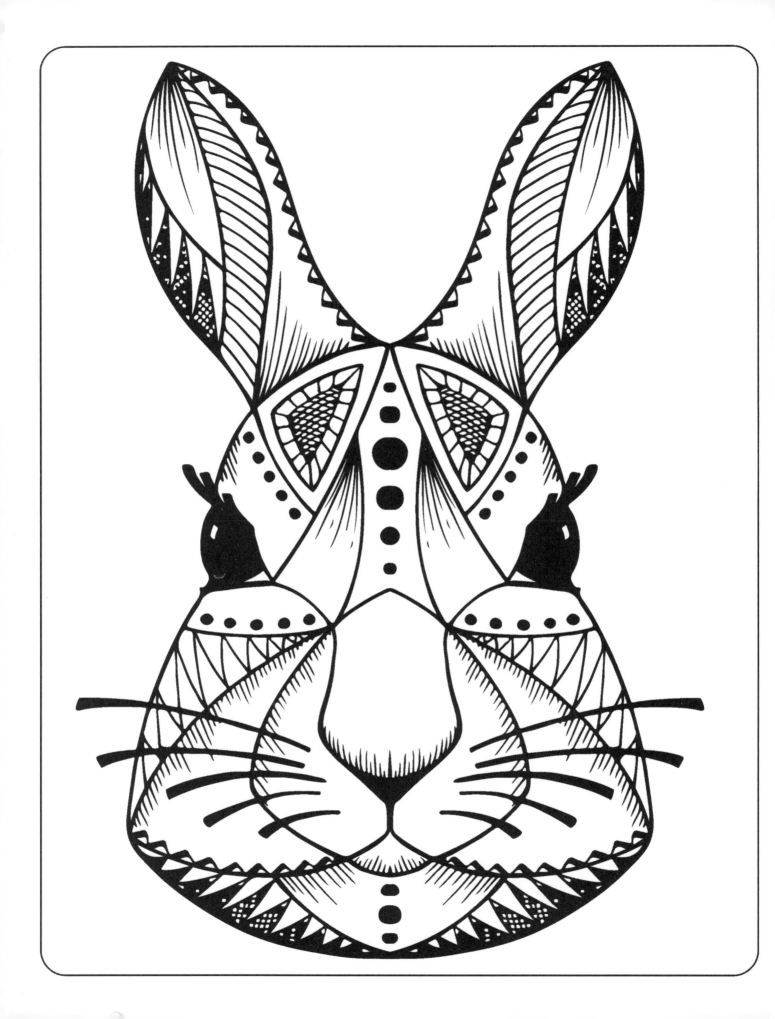